INSIGHTS
Joy

INSIGHTS
Joy

What the Bible Tells Us about Christian Joy

WILLIAM BARCLAY

SAINT ANDREW PRESS
Edinburgh

First published in 2009 by
SAINT ANDREW PRESS
121 George Street
Edinburgh EH2 4YN

ISBN 978 0 7152 0886 1

British Library Cataloguing in Publication Data
A catalogue record for this book is available from the British Library

It is the publisher's policy to only use papers that are natural and recyclable and that have been manufactured from timber grown in renewable, properly managed forests. All of the manufacturing processes of the papers are expected to conform to the environmental regulations of the country of origin.

Typeset by Waverley Typesetters, Fakenham
Printed and bound by Bell & Bain Ltd, Glasgow

Contents

Foreword

There are few things quite so funny as a lugubrious preacher talking about joy. Rikki Fulton made a highly successful second career out of it. The more his famous character, the Reverend I M Jolly, talked about Christian joy, the sadder, and funnier, he became. The humour lay in the disparity between what he said and the actuality of his face and voice. It was said of one real-life hangdog preacher that he often spoke about joy, 'but he forgot to tell his face'.

Professor William Barclay is no Rev I M Jolly. He was a warm, kindly man who was much beloved by his students. Oh, and he happened to be one of the finest Christian teachers and communicators of the twentieth century.

When the first series of Willie Barclay talks on television was launched, it was scoffed at for being everything television was supposed not to be in the brave new world. TV, we were told, was about moving images and not about talking heads. Audiences, said the critics, would not have the concentration span for a set of lectures. Not only that, Professor Barclay had not even had a 'make-over'!

Willie Barclay would not have allowed an image consultant near him.

The rest is history, or even mystery. It came to pass that an elderly man with a hearing aid, wearing a black gown and writing Greek words on a blackboard, captivated a growing television audience. Refusing to talk down to people, he explained complex theological concepts in a gravel-voiced Scottish accent. Without being at all simplistic, he de-mystified the closed language of academic theology, and, to use a phrase applied to Jesus, 'the common people heard him gladly'.

Scotland – not just churchgoing Scotland – was hooked. There was no point in visiting people on Sunday evenings when Willie Barclay was on the telly. His Bible commentaries and translations, published by Saint Andrew Press, sold many millions of copies. This wonderful new series, *Insights*, shows the ever-new appeal of biblical teaching well presented.

Professor Barclay doesn't confuse joy with positive thinking. As he expounds the New Testament teaching, he points out how Christian joy never evades tough realities. Talking of the paradox of blessedness, the good professor – who knew profound sadness in his own life – points out: 'To be chosen by God so often means at one and the same time a crown of joy and a cross of sorrow. The piercing truth is that God does not choose a person for ease and comfort and selfish joy but for a task that will take all that head and heart and hand can bring to it. *God chooses us in order to use us* … It is the paradox of blessedness that it confers on a person at one and the same time the greatest joy and the greatest task in all the world.'

Willie Barclay sets his face against gloomy Christianity. 'We are chosen for *joy*,' he insists. 'However hard the Christian way is, it is, both in the travelling and in the goal, the way of joy. There is always joy in doing the right thing. Christians are men and women of joy. A gloomy Christian is a contradiction in terms, and nothing in all religious history has done Christianity more harm than its connection with black clothes and long faces. It is true that Christians are sinners; but they are *redeemed* sinners, and therein lies their joy. How can any of us fail to be happy when we walk the way of life with Jesus?'

Move over, I M Jolly. Enjoy this book.

RON FERGUSON

Introduction

Jesus turned the water into wine

This is one of the most famous episodes in the Gospel of John. Yet, for many people, the details are vague and its meaning has lapsed into obscurity. Some people may know it as Jesus' first miracle and that it took place at a wedding, but there is so much more to it than that. William Barclay says that there are always two things to see in John's Gospel: the simple surface story and the deeper meaning beyond it. So he looks at the wedding story in stages to find the meanings.

First of all, he explains the background to help it to come alive. After all, this episode happened long ago and far away, set against a background and a culture of which many of us have only a passing knowledge. But Barclay tells us what we need to know so that the story can be viewed as if we were contemporary onlookers. We learn about the customs of Jewish weddings, including the information that wine was essential for a Jewish feast, and that the wine was served as two parts wine to three parts water.

Next, Barclay looks at what the story tells us about Jesus and his work. We learn that Jesus had maybe caused a problem for the wedding hosts because he arrived at the celebration with five disciples, whom he had only recently asked to follow him. There just wasn't enough wine to go around. But Jesus had a plan. Large water jars were filled to the brim with water and, when they drank from them, the guests were drinking beautiful wine. The people were enjoying themselves on a very happy occasion in the presence of a very special person.

Finally, Barclay reveals the hidden truth of the story: 'what John wants us to see here is not that Jesus once on a day turned some water pots of water into wine; he wants us to see that whenever Jesus comes into a person's life, there comes a new quality which is like turning water into wine.' With Jesus, life is 'thrilling and exhilarating'. This is Christian joy.

Insights: Joy contains other stories and passages from the New Testament on the theme of Christian joy — some of them familiar, some of them less so. In reading them, you will discover what sort of reactions a Christian should have to both the difficult times and the happy times.

The episodes and stories described in *Insights: Joy* all have a wider context, which you can find in Barclay's *New Daily Study Bible* series. Each book of the New Testament has its own writer, style of writing, historical background, original readership and so on. In reading about these, we can add to our understanding of the Bible. We hope you will be inspired to learn more about the New Testament through William Barclay's classic books. A list of them can be found at the end of this book.

The shepherd's joy

Luke 15:1–7

The tax-collectors and sinners were all coming near to Jesus to hear him, and the Pharisees and scribes were murmuring, saying, 'This man welcomes sinners and eats with them.'

He spoke this parable to them. 'What man of you,' he said, 'who has a hundred sheep, and who has lost one of them, does not leave the ninety-nine in the wilderness and go after the one that is lost until he finds it? And when he finds it, rejoicing he lays it on his shoulders; and when he comes home he calls together his friends and neighbours, saying to them, "Rejoice with me because I have found my sheep which was lost." I tell you that just so there will be joy in heaven over one sinner who repents more than over ninety-nine just people who have no need of repentance.'

THERE is no chapter of the New Testament so well known and so dearly loved as the fifteenth chapter of Luke's gospel. It has been called 'the gospel in the gospel', as if it contained the very distilled essence of the good news which Jesus came to tell.

These parables arose out of definite situations. It was an offence to the scribes and Pharisees that Jesus associated with men and women who, by the orthodox, were labelled as sinners. The Pharisees gave to people who did not keep the law a general classification. They called them *the People of the Land*; and there was a complete barrier between the Pharisees and the People of the Land. The Pharisaic regulations laid it down, 'When a man is one of the People of the Land, entrust no money to him, take no testimony from him, trust him with no secret, do not appoint him guardian of an orphan, do not make him the custodian of charitable funds, do not accompany him on a journey.' A Pharisee was forbidden to be the guest of any such man or to have him as his guest. He was even forbidden, so far as it was possible, to have any business dealings with him. It was the deliberate Pharisaic aim to avoid every contact with the people who did not observe the petty details of the law. Obviously, they would be shocked to the core at the way in which Jesus kept company with people who were not only rank outsiders but sinners, contact with whom would necessarily defile. We will understand these parables more fully if we remember that the strict Jews said, not 'There will be joy in heaven over one sinner who repents', but, 'There will be joy in heaven over one sinner who is obliterated before God.' They looked forward not to the saving but to the destruction of the sinner.

So Jesus told them the parable of the lost sheep and the shepherd's joy. The shepherd in Judaea had a hard and dangerous task. Pasture was scarce. The narrow central plateau was only a few miles wide, and then it plunged down to the wild cliffs and the terrible devastation of the desert. There were no restraining walls and the sheep would wander. George Adam Smith, an Old Testament scholar who travelled extensively in Palestine, wrote of the shepherd, 'On some high moor across which at night the hyaenas howl, when you meet him, sleepless, far-sighted, weather-beaten, armed, leaning on his staff and looking out over his scattered sheep, every one of them on his heart, you understand why the shepherd of Judaea sprang to the front in his people's history; why they gave his name to the king and made him the symbol of providence; why Christ took him as the type of self-sacrifice.'

The shepherd was personally responsible for the sheep. If a sheep was lost the shepherd must at least bring home the fleece to show how it had died. These shepherds were experts at tracking and could follow the straying sheep's footprints for miles across the hills. There was not a shepherd for whom it was not all in the day's work to risk his life for his sheep.

Many of the flocks were communal flocks, belonging not to individuals but to villages. There would be two or three shepherds in charge. Those whose flocks were safe would arrive home on time and bring news that one shepherd was still out on the mountainside searching for a sheep which was lost. The whole village would be upon the watch, and when, in the distance, they saw the shepherd striding home with the lost sheep across his shoulders, there would rise from the whole community a shout of joy and of thanksgiving.

That is the picture Jesus drew of God; that, said Jesus, is what God is like. God is as glad when a lost sinner is found as a shepherd is when a strayed sheep is brought home. As a great saint said, 'God, too, knows the joy of finding things that have gone lost.'

There is a wondrous thought here. It is the truly tremendous truth that God is kinder than men and women. The orthodox would write off the tax-collectors and the sinners as beyond the pale and as deserving of nothing but destruction; not so God. We may give up hope of a sinner; not so God. God loves those who never stray away; but in his heart there is the joy of joys when a lost one is found and comes home. It is 1,000 times easier to come back to God than to come home to the bleak criticism of our fellow human beings. F. W. Faber's hymn expresses this admirably:

Souls of men! why will ye scatter
Like a crowd of frightened sheep?
Foolish hearts! why will ye wander
From a love so true and deep?

Was there ever kindest shepherd
Half so gentle, half so sweet,
As the Saviour who would have us
Come and gather round his feet?

For the love of God is broader
Than the measure of man's mind;
And the heart of the Eternal
Is most wonderfully kind.

The life of Jesus' chosen people

John 15:11–17

> *'I have spoken these things to you that my joy might be in you, and that your joy might be complete. This is my commandment, that you love one another, as I have loved you. No one has greater love than this, that a man should lay down his life for his friend. You are my friends, if you do what I command you. I no longer call you slaves, because the slave does not know what his master is doing. I have called you friends because I have made known to you everything that I heard from my Father. You have not chosen me, but I have chosen you, and I have appointed you to go out and to bear fruit, of such a kind that it will remain. I have done so, so that the Father will give you whatever you ask him in my name. These are my orders to you, that you love one another.'*

THE central words of this passage are those in which Jesus says that his disciples have not chosen him, but he has chosen them. It was not we who chose God, but God who, in his grace, approached us with a call and an offer made out of his love.

Out of this passage, we can compile a list of things for which we are chosen and to which we are called.

(1) We are chosen for *joy*. However hard the Christian way is, it is, both in the travelling and in the goal, the way of joy. There is always a joy in doing the right thing. Christians are men and women of joy. A gloomy Christian is a contradiction in terms, and nothing in all religious history has done Christianity more harm than its connection with black clothes and long faces. It is true that Christians are sinners; but they are *redeemed* sinners, and therein lies their joy. How can any of us fail to be happy when we walk the ways of life with Jesus?

(2) We are chosen for *love*. We are sent out into the world to love one another. Sometimes we live as if we were sent into the world to compete with one another, or to dispute with one another, or even to quarrel with one another. But Christians are to live in such a way that they show what is meant by loving our neighbours. It is here that Jesus makes another of his great claims. If we ask him: 'What right have you to demand that we love one another?', his answer is: 'No one can show greater love than to lay down his life for his friends – and I did that.' Many tell people to love each other, when their whole lives are a demonstration that that is the last thing they do themselves. Jesus gave us a commandment which he had himself first fulfilled.

(3) Jesus called us to be *his friends*. He tells his disciples that he does not call them slaves any more; he calls them friends. Now that is a saying which would be even greater to those who heard it for the first time than it is to us. *Doulos*, the slave, the servant of God, was no title of shame; it was a title of the highest honour. Moses was the *doulos* of God (Deuteronomy 34:5); so was Joshua (Joshua 24:29); so was David (Psalm 89:20). It is a title which Paul counted it an

honour to use (Titus 1:1); and so did James (James 1:1). The greatest men in the past had been proud to be called the *douloi*, the slaves of God. And Jesus says: 'I have something greater for you yet: you are no longer *slaves; you are friends*.' Christ offers an intimacy with God which not even the greatest men and women knew before he came into the world.

The idea of being the friend of God also has a background. Abraham was the *friend* of God (Isaiah 41:8). In Wisdom 7:27, Wisdom is said to make people the friends of God. But this phrase is lit up by a custom practised at the courts both of the Roman emperors and of kings in the middle east. At these courts, there was a very select group called *the friends of the king*, or *the friends of the emperor*. At all times, they had access to the king; they even had the right to come to his bedchamber at the beginning of the day. He talked to them before he talked to his generals, his rulers and his statesmen. The friends of the king were those who had the closest and the most intimate connection with him.

Jesus called us to be his friends and the friends of God. That is a tremendous offer. It means that no longer do we need to gaze longingly at God from afar; we are not like slaves who have no right whatsoever to enter into the presence of the master; we are not like a crowd whose only glimpse of the king is in the passing on some state occasion. Jesus gave us this intimacy with God, so that he is no longer a distant stranger but our close friend.

The paradox of blessedness

Luke 1:39–45

> *In those days Mary arose and went eagerly to the hill country, to a city of Judah, and went into the house of Zacharias and greeted Elizabeth. When Elizabeth heard Mary's greeting the babe leaped in her womb and Elizabeth was filled with the Holy Spirit, and she lifted up her voice with a great cry and said, 'Blessed are you among women and blessed is the fruit of your womb. Why has this been granted to me – that the mother of my Lord should come to me? For – look you – when the voice of your greeting came to my ears the babe in my womb leaped with exultation. Blessed is she who believed that the things spoken to her from the Lord would find their fulfilment.'*

THIS is a kind of lyrical song on the blessedness of Mary. Nowhere can we better see the paradox of blessedness than in her life. To Mary was granted the blessedness of being the mother of the Son of God. Well might her heart be filled with a wondering, tremulous joy at so great a privilege. Yet that very blessedness was to be a sword to pierce her heart. It meant that some day she would see her son hanging on a cross.

To be chosen by God so often means at one and the same time a crown of joy and cross of sorrow. The piercing truth is that God does not choose a person for ease and comfort and selfish joy but for a task that will take all that head and heart and hand can bring to it. *God chooses us in order to use us*. When Joan of Arc knew that her time was short she prayed, 'I shall only last a year; use me as you can.' When that is realized, the sorrows and hardships that serving God may bring are not matters for lamentation; they are our glory, for all is suffered for God.

When Richard Cameron, the Covenanter, was caught by the dragoons they killed him. He had very beautiful hands and they cut them off and sent them to his father with a message asking if he recognized them. 'They are my son's,' he said, 'my own dear son's. Good is the will of the Lord who can never wrong me or mine.' The shadows of life were lit by the sense that they, too, were in the plan of God. A great Spanish saint prayed for his people, 'May God deny you peace and give you glory.' One great preacher said, 'Jesus Christ came not to make life easy but to make men great.'

It is the paradox of blessedness that it confers on a person at one and the same time the greatest joy and the greatest task in all the world.

The joyous company

Mark 2:18–20

> *The disciples of John were in the habit of fasting, as were the Pharisees. So they came to Jesus and said, 'Why do John's disciples and the disciples of the Pharisees fast, while your disciples do not?' 'Surely', Jesus said to them, 'his closest friends cannot fast while the bridegroom is still with them? So long as they have the bridegroom they do not fast. But the days will come when some day the bridegroom will be taken away from them – and then, in that day, they will fast.'*

WITH the stricter Jews, fasting was a regular practice. In Judaism there was only one day in all the year that was a compulsory fast, and that was the Day of Atonement. The day when the nation confessed and was forgiven its sin was The Fast *par excellence*. But the stricter Jews fasted on two days every week, on Mondays and Thursdays. It is to be noted that fasting was not as serious as it sounds, for the fast lasted from 6 am to 6 pm and after that normal food could be eaten.

Jesus is not against fasting as such. There are very good reasons why people might fast. They might deny themselves things they like for the sake of *discipline*, to be certain that they have control over them and not the other way about, to make sure that they never grow to love them so well that they cannot give them up. They might deny themselves comforts and pleasant things so that, after such self-denial, they might appreciate them all the more. One of the best ways to learn to value our homes is to have to stay away from home for a time; and one of the best ways to appreciate God's gifts is to do without them for a period.

These are good reasons for fasting. The trouble about the Pharisees was that in far too many cases their fasting was for self-display. It was to call the attention of *others* to their goodness. They actually whitened their faces and went about with dishevelled garments on their fast days so that no one could miss the fact that they were fasting and so that everyone would see and admire their devotion. It was to call the attention of *God* to their piety. They felt that this special act of extra piety would bring them to the notice of God. Their fasting was a ritual and a self-displaying ritual at that. To be of any value, fasting must not be the result of a ritual; it must be the expression of a feeling in the heart.

Jesus used a vivid picture to tell the Pharisees why his disciples did not fast. After a Jewish wedding, the couple did not go away for a honeymoon; they stayed at home. For a week or so, open house was kept and there was continual feasting and rejoicing. In lives that were hard, a wedding week was the happiest time. To that week of happiness were invited the closest friends of the bride and the bridegroom; and they were called by the name *children of the bride-chamber*. Jesus likened his little company to men who were children of the bridechamber, chosen guests at a wedding feast. There was actually a Rabbinic ruling which said, 'All in attendance on the bridegroom are relieved of all religious observances which would lessen their joy.' The wedding guests were actually exempt from all fasting.

This incident tells us that the characteristic Christian attitude to life is joy. The discovery of Christ and the company of Christ are the key to happiness. There was a Japanese criminal called Tokichi Ishii. He was utterly pitiless; he had brutally and callously murdered men, women and children in his career of crime. He was captured and imprisoned. Two Canadian ladies visited the prison. He could not be induced even to speak; he only glowered at them with the face of a wild animal. When they left, they left with him a copy of the Bible in the faint hope that he might read it. He read it, and the story of the crucifixion made him a changed man. Later when the jailer came to lead the doomed man to the gallows, he found not the surly, hardened brute he expected, but a smiling, radiant man, for Ishii the murderer had been born again. The mark of his rebirth was a smiling radiance. The life that is lived in Christ cannot be lived other than in joy.

But the story ends with a foreboding cloud across the sky. No doubt when Jesus spoke of the day when the bridegroom would be taken away his friends did not at the moment see the meaning of it. But here, right at the beginning, Jesus saw the cross ahead. Death did not take him unawares; even now he had counted the cost and chosen the way. Here is courage; here is the picture of a man who would not be deflected from the road at whose end there loomed a cross.

The bliss of the broken heart

Matthew 5:4

'Blessed are those who mourn, for they will be comforted.'

It is first of all to be noted about this beatitude that the Greek word for *to mourn*, used here, is the strongest word for mourning in the Greek language. It is the word which is used for mourning for the dead, for the passionate lament for one who was loved. In the Septuagint, the Greek version of the Old Testament, it is the word which is used of Jacob's grief when he believed that Joseph, his son, was dead (Genesis 37:34). It is defined as the kind of grief which takes such a hold that it cannot be hidden. It is not only the sorrow which brings an ache to the heart; it is the sorrow which brings the unrestrainable tears to the eyes. Here then indeed is an amazing kind of bliss:

> *Blessed are those who mourn like those mourning for the dead.*

There are three ways in which this beatitude can be taken.

(1) It can be taken quite literally: blessed are those who have endured the bitterest sorrow that life can bring. The

Arabs have a proverb: 'All sunshine makes a desert.' The land on which the sun always shines will soon become an arid place in which no fruit will grow. There are certain things which only the rains will produce, and certain experiences which can only come out of sorrow.

Sorrow can do two things for us. It can show us, as nothing else can, the essential kindness of others; and it can show us, as nothing else can, the comfort and the compassion of God. So many people in the hour of their sorrow have discovered other people and God as never before. When things go well, it is possible to live for years on the surface of things; but when sorrow comes, we are driven to the deep things of life, and, if we accept it aright, a new strength and beauty will enter into our souls.

(2) Some people have taken this beatitude to mean:

> *Blessed are those who are desperately sorry for the sorrow and the suffering of this world.*

It is always right to be detached from *things*, but it is never right to be detached *from people*. This world would have been a very much poorer place if there had not been those who cared intensely about the sorrows and the sufferings of others.

Through his work on the factory and coal mining acts in the nineteenth century, Lord Shaftesbury probably did more for ordinary working men and women and for little children than any social reformer ever did. It all began very simply. When he was a boy at Harrow, he was going along the street one day, and he met a pauper's funeral. The coffin was a shoddy, ill-made box. It was on a hand-barrow. The barrow was being pushed by a quartet of men who were drunk; and as they pushed the barrow along, they were singing ribald songs, and joking and jesting among themselves. As they pushed the barrow up the hill, the box, which was the coffin, fell off the barrow and burst open. Some people would have thought the whole business a good joke; some would have turned away in fastidious disgust; some would have shrugged their shoulders and would have felt that it had nothing to do with them, although it might be a pity that such things should happen. The young Shaftesbury saw it and said to himself: 'When I grow up, I'm going to give my life to see that things like that don't happen.' So he dedicated his life to caring for others.

Christianity *is* caring. This beatitude does mean: blessed are those who care intensely for the sufferings, and for the sorrows, and for the needs of others.

(3) No doubt both these thoughts are in this beatitude, but its main thought undoubtedly is: blessed are those who are desperately sorry for their own sin and their own unworthiness.

The very first word of the message of Jesus was: 'Repent!' We cannot repent unless we are sorry for our sins. The thing which really changes people is when they suddenly come up against something which opens their eyes to what sin is and to what sin does. A boy or a girl may go his or her own way, and may never think of effects and consequences; and then some day something happens and that boy or girl sees the stricken look in a father's or a mother's eyes, and suddenly sin is seen for what it is.

That is what the cross does for us. As we look at the cross, we are bound to say: 'That is what sin can do. Sin can take the loveliest life in all the world and smash it on a cross.' One of the great functions of the cross is to open the eyes of men and women to the horror of sin. And when they see sin in all its horror, they cannot do anything else but experience intense sorrow for their sin.

Christianity begins with a sense of sin. Blessed are those who are intensely sorry for their sin, those who are heart-broken for what their sin has done to God and to Jesus Christ, those who see the cross and who are appalled by the havoc wrought by sin.

It is the man or woman who has that experience who will indeed be comforted; for that experience is what we call penitence, and the broken and the contrite heart God will never despise (Psalm 51:17). The way to the joy of forgiveness is through the desperate sorrow of the broken heart.

The real meaning of the second beatitude is:

> O THE BLISS OF THOSE WHOSE HEARTS ARE BROKEN FOR THE WORLD'S SUFFERING AND FOR THEIR OWN SIN, FOR OUT OF THEIR SORROW THEY WILL FIND THE JOY OF GOD!

15

The happy ending

Luke 24:50–3

> *Jesus led them out as far as Bethany; and he raised his hands and blessed them; and as he was blessing them he parted from them, and was borne up into heaven. And when they had worshipped him they returned to Jerusalem with great joy; and they were continually in the Temple praising God.*

THE ascension must always remain a mystery, for it attempts to put into words what is beyond words and to describe what is beyond description. But that something of this order should happen was essential. It was unthinkable that the appearances of Jesus should grow fewer and fewer until finally they petered out. That would have effectively wrecked the disciples' faith. There had to come a day of dividing when the Jesus of earth finally became the Christ of heaven. But to the disciples the ascension was obviously three things.

(1) It was *an ending*. The days when their faith was faith in a flesh-and-blood person and depended on his flesh-and-blood presence were over. Now they were linked to someone who was forever independent of space and time.

(2) Equally it was a *beginning*. The disciples did not leave the scene heartbroken; they left it with great joy, because

now they knew that they had a Master from whom nothing could separate them any more. In the words of J. G. Whittier's hymn:

I know not where his islands lift
Their fronded palms in air;
I only know I cannot drift
Beyond his love and care.

'I am sure', said Paul, 'that nothing – nothing in life or death – can separate us from the love of God in Christ Jesus our Lord' (cf. Romans 8:38–9).

(3) Further, the ascension gave the disciples the certainty that they had *a friend, not only on earth, but in heaven*. Surely it is the most precious thing of all to know that in heaven there awaits us that self-same Jesus who on earth was wondrous kind. To die is not to go out into the dark; it is to go to him.

So they went back to Jerusalem, and they were continually in the Temple praising God. It is not by accident that Luke's gospel ends where it began – in the house of God.

The marks of the Christian life (1)

Philippians 4:4–5

> *Rejoice in the Lord at all times. I will say it again – rejoice! Let your gracious gentleness be known to all men. The Lord is near.*

PAUL sets before the Philippians two great qualities of the Christian life.

(1) The first is the quality of joy. 'Rejoice . . . I will say it again – rejoice!' It is as if, having said 'Rejoice!', a picture of all that was to come flashed into his mind. He himself was lying in prison with almost certain death awaiting him; the Philippians were setting out on the Christian way, and dark days, dangers and persecutions inevitably lay ahead. So Paul says: 'I know what I'm saying. I've thought of everything that can possibly happen. And still I say it – Rejoice!' Christian joy is independent of all things on earth because it has its source in the continual presence of Christ. Two people who love each other are always happy when they are together, no matter where they are. Christians can never lose their joy because they can never lose Christ.

(2) Paul goes on, as the Authorized Version has it: 'Let your moderation be known to all men.' The word (*epieikeia*)

translated as *moderation* is one of the most untranslatable of all Greek words. The difficulty can be seen by the number of translations given of it. Wyclif translates it as *patience*; Tyndale, *softness*; Cranmer, *softness*; the Geneva Bible, *the patient mind*; the Rheims Bible, *modesty*; the Revised Version, *forbearance* (in the margin *gentleness*); Moffatt, *forbearance*; Weymouth, the *forbearing spirit*; the New English Bible, *magnanimity*. In his translation of the New Testament, Charles Kingsley Williams has: 'Let all the world know that you will *meet a man half-way*.'

The Greeks themselves explained this word as 'justice and something better than justice'. They said that *epieikeia* ought to come in when strict justice became unjust because of its generality. There may be individual instances where a perfectly just law becomes unjust or where justice is not the same thing as fairness. People have the quality of *epieikeia* if they know when *not* to apply the strict letter of the law, when to relax justice and introduce mercy.

Let us take a simple example which every teacher encounters almost every day. Here are two students. We correct their examination papers. We apply justice and find that one has 80 per cent and the other 50 per cent. But we go a little further and find that the one who got 80 per cent has been able to work in ideal conditions with books, leisure and peace to study, while the one who got 50 per cent struggles to cope financially and has inadequate equipment, or has been ill, or has recently come through some time of sorrow or strain. In justice, this student deserves 50 per cent and no more; but *epieikeia* will value the examination paper far higher than that.

Epieikeia is the quality of someone who knows that regulations are not the last word and knows when not to apply the letter of the law. A kirk session may sit with the book of practice and procedure on the table in front of it and take every one of its decisions in strict accordance with the law of the church; but there are times when the Christian treatment of some situation demands that that book of practice and procedure should not be regarded as the last word.

Christians, as Paul sees it, are men and women who know that there is something beyond justice. When the woman taken in adultery was brought before him, Jesus could have applied the letter of the law, according to which she should have been stoned to death; but he went beyond justice. As far as justice goes, there is not one of us who deserves anything other than the condemnation of God; but God goes far beyond justice. Paul lays it down that the mark of Christians in their personal relationships with others must be that they know when to insist on justice and when to remember that there is something beyond justice.

Why should we be like this? Why should we have this joy and gracious gentleness in our lives? Because, says Paul, the Lord is at hand. If we remember the coming triumph of Christ, we can never lose our hope and our joy. If we remember that life is short, we will not want to enforce the stern justice which so often divides people but will want to deal with others in love, as we hope that God will deal with us. Justice is human, but *epieikeia* is divine.

Christians and their neighbours

Romans 12:15

> *Rejoice with those who rejoice, and weep with those who weep.*

We are to rejoice with those who rejoice, and to weep with those who weep. There are few bonds like that of a common sorrow. A writer tells the story of a black American woman. A lady in Charleston met the black servant of a neighbour. 'I'm sorry to hear of your Aunt Lucy's death,' she said. 'You must miss her greatly. You were such friends.' 'Yes,' said the servant, 'I'm sorry she died. But we weren't friends.' 'Why,' said the lady, 'I thought you were. I've seen you laughing and talking together lots of times.' 'Yes. That's so,' came the reply. 'We've laughed together, and we've talked together, but we were just acquaintances. You see, Miss Ruth, we never shed any tears. Folks have got to cry together before they are friends.'

The bond of tears is the strongest of all. And yet it is much easier to weep with those who weep than it is to rejoice with those who rejoice. Long ago, in the fourth century, the Church father John Chrysostom wrote on this passage: 'It requires more of a high Christian temper to rejoice with them that do rejoice than to weep with them that weep. For this nature itself fulfils perfectly; and there is none so hard-hearted as not to weep over him that is in calamity; but the other requires a very noble soul, so as not only to keep from envying, but even to feel pleasure with the person who is in esteem.' It is, indeed, more difficult to congratulate others on their success, especially if their success involves disappointment to us, than it is to sympathize with their sorrow and their loss. It is only when self is dead that we can take as much joy in the success of others as in our own.

Godly sorrow and Godly joy

2 Corinthians 7:5–16

> *For when we arrived in Macedonia we could find no rest for our body, but we were sore pressed on every side. There were wars without and fears within. But he who comforts the lowly comforted us – I mean God – by the arrival of Titus. We found this comfort not only in his arrival, but in the comfort which he found among you, for he brought news of your longing to see me, of your grief for the past situation, of your zeal to show your loyalty to me. The consequence was that my gladness was greater than my troubles. For if I grieved you with the letter I sent you, I am not sorry that I sent it, although, to tell the truth, I was sorry; for I see that that letter, if it was only for a time, did grieve you. Now I am glad, not that you were grieved, but that your grief was the way to repentance. It was a godly grief that came to you, so that you have lost nothing through our action, for godly grief produces repentance which leads to salvation and which no man ever regrets. But worldly grief produces death. Look now! This very thing, this godly grief – see what earnest longing it produced in you, what a desire to set yourselves right, what vexation at what you had done, what fear, what yearning, what zeal, what steps to inflict condign [severe] punishment on*

the man who deserved it! You have shown yourselves pure in this matter. If I did indeed write to you, it was not for the sake of him who committed the wrong, nor for the sake of him who was wronged; it was to make quite clear to you in the sight of God the earnestness you really possessed for us. Because of this, we have been comforted. In addition to this comfort which came to us, we rejoiced with still more overflowing joy in the joy of Titus, because his spirit was refreshed by the way in which you all treated him. For if I did rather boast about him, I was not put to shame, but just as everything we have said to you was spoken with truth, so too our boast about Titus was proved to be the truth. And his heart goes out overflowingly to you when he remembers what obedience you showed, how you received him with fear and trembling. I am glad that in everything I am in good heart about you.

THE connection of this section really goes as far back as 2:12–13, for it is there that Paul tells how in Troas he had no rest because he did not know how the Corinthian situation had developed, and how he had set out to Macedonia to meet Titus to get the news as quickly as possible. Let us again remember the circumstances. Things had gone wrong in Corinth. In an attempt to mend them, Paul had paid a flying visit which only made them worse and nearly broke his heart. After the failure of the visit, he had despatched Titus with a letter of quite exceptional sternness and severity. He was so worried about the outcome of the whole unhappy business that he was quite unable to rest at Troas, although there was much there that he might have done, so he set out to meet Titus to get the news as quickly as possible. He met Titus somewhere in Macedonia and learned to his overflowing joy that the trouble was over, the divisions were healed and all was well. That is the background of events against which this passage must be read, and it makes it very rich.

It tells us certain things about Paul's whole method and outlook on rebuke.

(1) He was quite clear that there came a time when rebuke was necessary. It often happens that those who seek an easy peace find in the end nothing but trouble. People who allow a dangerous situation to develop because they shrink from dealing with it, parents who exercise no discipline because they fear unpleasantness, those who will not grasp the nettle of danger because they want to find the flower of safety, in the end simply pile up greater trouble for themselves. Trouble is like disease. If it is dealt with at the right time, it can often easily be eradicated; if not, it can become an incurable growth.

(2) Even admitting all that, the last thing Paul wished was to rebuke. He did it only because he felt compelled to do so and took no pleasure whatever in inflicting pain. There are those who take a sadistic pleasure in seeing someone wince beneath the lash of their tongue, who pride themselves on being candid when they are only being rude, and on being blunt when they are only being boorish. It is the simple fact that the rebuke which is given with a certain relish will never prove as effective as the rebuke which is obviously unwillingly given only because there is no alternative.

(3) Further, Paul's sole object in giving rebuke was to enable people to be what they ought to be. By his rebuke, he wished the Corinthians to see just how serious he was in his concern for them, in spite of their disobedience and their

troublemaking. Such a course might, for the moment, cause pain, but its ultimate purpose was not the pain; it was not to knock them down, but to lift them up; it was not to discourage them, but to encourage them; it was not simply to eradicate the evil, but to make the good grow.

This passage tells us also of three great human joys.

(1) There breathes through it all the joy of reconciliation, the healed split and the mended quarrel. We all remember times in childhood when we had done something wrong and there was a barrier between us and our parents. We all know that that can still happen between us and those we love. And we all know the flood of relief and the happiness when the barriers are gone and we are at one again with those we love. In the last analysis, people who cherish bitterness hurt no one more than they hurt themselves.

(2) There is the joy of seeing someone in whom you believe justifying that belief. Paul had given Titus a good reference, and Titus had gone to face a very difficult situation. Paul was overjoyed that Titus had justified his confidence in him and proved his words true. Nothing brings deeper satisfaction than knowing that our own sons and daughters in the faith do well. The deepest joy that sons or daughters or scholars or students can bring to parents or teachers is to demonstrate that they are as good as the parents or the teachers believe them to be. Life's deepest tragedy lies in disappointed hopes, and life's greatest joy comes in hopes that are fulfilled.

(3) There is the joy of seeing someone you love welcomed and well treated. It is a fact of life that kindness shown to those we love moves us even more deeply than kindness shown to ourselves. What is true of us is true of God. That is

why we can best show our love of God by loving one another. The thing that delights the heart of God is to see one of his children kindly treated. Inasmuch as we do it to them, we do it to him.

This passage also draws one of the most important distinctions in life. It draws the distinction between *godly* and *worldly* sorrow.

(1) A godly sorrow produces a true repentance, and a true repentance is one which demonstrates its sorrow by its actions. The Corinthians proved their repentance by doing everything they could to mend the wretched situation that their thoughtless conduct had produced. Now they hated the sin they had committed, and even hated themselves for committing it, and they worked hard to atone for it.

(2) A worldly sorrow is not really sorrow at all in one sense, for it is not sorrow for its sin or for the hurt it may have caused others; it is only resentment that it has been found out. If it got the chance to do the same thing again and thought it could escape the consequences, it would do it. A godly sorrow is a sorrow which has come to see the wrongness of the thing it did. It is not just the consequences of the thing it regrets; it hates the thing itself. We must be very careful that our sorrow for sin is not merely sorrow that we have been found out, but sorrow which, seeing the evil of the sinful thing, is determined never to do it again and has dedicated the rest of its life to atone, by God's grace, for what it has done.

The indestructible joy

Philippians 3:1

> *As for what remains, my brothers, rejoice in the Lord. It is no trouble to me to write the same things to you, and for you it is safe.*

PAUL sets down two very important things.

(1) He sets down what we might call the indestructibility of Christian joy. He must have felt that he had been setting a high challenge before the Philippian church. For them there was the possibility of the same kind of persecution, and even the same kind of death, as threatened himself. From one point of view, it looked as if Christianity was a grim challenge. But, in it and beyond it all, there was joy. 'No one', said Jesus, 'will take your joy from you' (John 16:22).

There is a certain indestructibility in Christian joy, and it is so because Christian joy is *in the Lord*. Its basis is that Christians live forever in the presence of Jesus Christ. They can lose everything, and they can lose everyone, but they can never lose Christ. And, therefore, even in circumstances where joy would seem to be impossible and there seems to be nothing but pain and discomfort, Christian joy remains, because not all the threats and terrors and discomforts of life can separate Christians from the love of God in Christ Jesus their Lord (Romans 8:35–9).

In 1756, a letter came to the Methodist John Wesley from a father who had a wayward son. When the revival swept England, the son was in York prison. 'It pleased God', wrote the father, 'not to cut him off in his sins. He gave him time to repent; and not only so, but a heart to repent.' The boy was condemned to death for his misdeeds, and the father's letter goes on: 'His peace increased daily, until on Saturday, the he was to die, he came out of the condemned-room, tithed in his shroud, and went into the cart. As he went on, the cheerfulness and composure of his countenance were amazing to all the spectators.' The young man had found a joy which not even the scaffold could take away.

It often happens that we can stand the great sorrows and the great trials of life but are quite unable to cope with what are almost minor inconveniences. But this Christian joy enables us to accept even these with a smile. John Nelson was one of John Wesley's most famous early preachers. He and Wesley carried out a mission in Cornwall, near Land's End, and Nelson writes about it. 'All that time, Mr Wesley and I lay on the floor: he had my greatcoat for a pillow, and I had Burkitt's notes on the New Testament for mine. After being here near three weeks, one morning about three o'clock Mr Wesley turned over, and, finding me awake, clapped me on the side, saying: "Brother Nelson, let us be of good cheer: I have one whole side yet, for the skin is off but on one side!"' They had little enough even to eat. One morning, Wesley had preached with great effect: 'As we returned, Mr Wesley stopped his horse to pick the blackberries, saying: "Brother Nelson, we ought to be thankful that there are plenty blackberries; for this is the best country I ever saw for getting a stomach, but the worst I ever saw for getting food!"' Christian Joy made Wesley able to accept the great blows of life and also to greet the lesser discomforts with humour. If Christians really walk with Christ, they walk with joy.

(2) Here also, Paul sets down what we might call the necessity of repetition. He says that he proposes to write things to them that he has written before. This is interesting, for it must mean that Paul had written other letters to the Philippians which have not survived. This is nothing to be surprised at. Paul was writing letters from AD 48 to AD 64 – sixteen years – but we possess only thirteen of them. Unless there were long periods when he never put pen to paper, there must have been many more letters which are now lost.

Like any good teacher, Paul was never afraid of repetition. It may well be that one of our faults is our desire for novelty. The great saving truths of Christianity do not change, and we cannot hear them too often. We do not tire of the foods which are the essentials of life. We expect to eat bread and to drink water every day, and we must listen again and again to the truth which is the bread and the water of life. No teacher must find it a trouble to go over the great basic truths of the Christian faith again and again; for that is the way to ensure the safety of the hearers. We may enjoy the 'fancy things' at meal times, but it is the basic foods on which we live. Preaching and teaching and studying the side issues may be attractive, and these have their place; but the fundamental truths can neither be spoken nor heard too often for the safety of our souls.

The peril of Christian freedom

Romans 14:17–20

> *Do not allow that good gift of freedom which you possess to become a thing which gets you into disrepute. For the kingdom of God does not consist of food and drink, but of righteousness and peace and joy, which are the gifts of the Holy Spirit. For the man who rules his life by this principle, and so becomes the slave of Christ, is well-pleasing to God and approved by men. So, then, let it be the things that make for peace that we pursue, and the things which build up one another. Do not destroy God's work for the sake of food. True, all things are pure; but it is wrong for a man to make life's road more difficult for someone else through what he eats.*

In essence, Paul is here dealing with the peril and the abuse of Christian freedom. To Jews, Christian freedom had its dangers. All their lives, they had been surrounded by a multiplicity of rules and regulations. So many things were unclean and so many were clean. So many animals might not be eaten; so many purity laws must be observed. When Jews came into Christianity, they found that all these rules and regulations were abolished at one stroke, and the danger was that they might interpret Christianity as a freedom to do exactly as they liked. We must remember that Christian freedom and Christian love go hand in hand; we must hold fast to the truth that Christian freedom and love for one another are bound up together.

Paul reminds his people that Christianity does not consist in eating and drinking what one likes. It consists in three great things, all of which are essentially *unselfish* things.

(1) There is *righteousness*, and this consists in giving to others and to God what is their due. Now, the very first thing that is due to other people in the Christian life is sympathy and consideration; the moment we become Christians, the feelings of others become *more* important than our own. Christianity means putting others first and self last. We cannot give to others what is due to them and do what we like.

(2) There is *peace*. In the New Testament, peace does not mean simply absence of trouble; it is not a negative thing, but is intensely positive; it means everything that makes for our highest good. The Jews themselves often thought of peace as a state of right relationships between individuals. If we insist that Christian freedom means doing what we like, that is precisely the state we can never attain. Christianity consists entirely in *personal relationships* to other people and to God. The unrestrained freedom of Christian liberty is conditioned by the Christian obligation to live in a right relationship, in peace, with one another.

(3) There is *joy*. Christian joy can never be a selfish thing. It does not consist in making ourselves happy; it consists in making others happy. A so-called happiness which made someone else distressed would not be Christian. If anyone, in the search for happiness, brings a hurt heart and a wounded conscience to someone else, the ultimate end

of that person's search will be not joy but sorrow. Christian joy is not individualistic; it is interdependent. Joy comes to Christians only when they bring joy to others, even if it costs them personal limitation.

When we follow this principle, we become the slaves of Christ. Here is the essence of the matter. Christian freedom means that we are free to do not what we like but what Christ likes. Without Christ, we are all slaves to our habits, our pleasures and our indulgences. We are not really doing what we like. We are doing what the things that have us in their grip make us do. Once the power of Christ enters into us, we take control of ourselves – and then, and only then, real freedom enters our lives. Then we are free not to treat others and not to live life as our own selfish human nature would have us do; we are free to show to everyone the same attitude of love as Jesus showed.

Paul ends by setting out the Christian aim within the fellowship. (1) It is the aim of *peace*; the aim that the members of the fellowship should be in a right relationship with each other. A church where there is strife and contention, quarrels and bitterness, divisions and disagreements, has lost all right to the name of church. It is not a fragment of the kingdom of heaven; it is simply an earthbound society. (2) It is the aim of *upbuilding*. The picture of the church as a building runs through the New Testament. The members are stones within the building. Anything which loosens the fabric of the church is against God; anything which makes that fabric stronger and more secure is of God.

The tragedy is that in so many cases it is little unimportant things which disturb the peace of the fellowship – matters of law, procedure, precedent and prestige. A new age would dawn in the Church if we remembered that our rights are far less important than our obligations, if we remembered that, while we possess Christian liberty, it is always an offence to use it as if it conferred upon us the right to grieve the heart and conscience of someone else. Unless a church is a body of people who, in love, consider one another, it is not a church at all.

The marks of the Christian life (2)

Christian Joy

Philippians 1:3–11

In all my remembrance of you I thank my God for you, and always in every one of my prayers I pray for you with joy, because you have been in partnership with me for the furtherance of the gospel from the first day until now, and of this I am confident, that he who began a good work in you will complete it so that you may be ready for the day of Jesus Christ. And it is right for me to feel like this about you, because I have you in my heart, because all of you are partners in grace with me, both in my hands, and in my defence and confirmation of the gospel. God is my witness how I yearn for you all with the very compassion of Christ Jesus. And this I pray, that your love for each other may continue to abound more and more in all fullness of knowledge and in all sensitiveness of perception, that you may test the things which differ, that you may be yourselves pure and that you may cause no other to stumble, in preparation for the day of Christ, because you have been filled with the fruit which the righteousness which comes through Jesus Christ produces, and which issues in glory and praise to God.

It is a lovely thing when, as Charles Ellicott, the nineteenth-century New Testament scholar and Bishop of Gloucester, puts it, remembrance and gratitude are bound up together. In our personal relationships, it is a great thing to have nothing but happy memories; and that was how Paul was with the Christians at Philippi. To remember brought no regrets, only happiness.

In this passage, the marks of the Christian life are set out.

There is *Christian joy*. It is with joy that Paul prays for his friends. The letter to the Philippians has been called the *Epistle of Joy*. The eighteenth-century German theologian Johannes Bengel, in his terse Latin, commented: '*Summa epistolae gaudeo – gaudete*.' 'The whole point of the letter is I rejoice; you rejoice.' Let us look at the picture of Christian joy which this letter paints.

(1) In 1:4, there is the joy of *Christian prayer*, the joy of bringing those we love to the mercy seat of God.

George Reindrop, in his book *No Common Task*, tells how a nurse once taught a man to pray and in doing so changed his whole life, until a dull, disgruntled and dispirited individual became a man of joy. The nurse showed how it is possible to use the hands as a scheme of prayer. Each finger stood for someone. Her thumb was nearest to her, and it reminded her to pray for those who were closest to her. The second finger was used for pointing, and it stood for all her teachers in school and in the hospital. The third finger was the tallest, and it stood for the VIPs, the leaders in every sphere of life. The fourth finger was the weakest, as every pianist knows, and it stood for those who were in trouble and in pain. The little finger was the smallest and the least important, and to the nurse it stood for herself.

There must always be a deep joy and peace in bringing our loved ones and others to God in prayer.

(2) There is the joy that *Jesus Christ is preached* (1:18). When we enjoy a great blessing, surely our first instinct must be to share it; and there is joy in thinking of the gospel being preached all over the world, so that at first one person and then another and another is brought within the love of Christ.

(3) There is the joy of *faith* (1:25). If Christianity does not make us happy, it will not make us anything at all. Christianity should never be a cause of anguish. The psalmist said: 'Look to him, and be radiant' (Psalm 34:5). When Moses came down from the mountain top, his face shone. Christianity is the faith of the happy heart and the shining face.

(4) There is the joy of seeing *Christians in fellowship together* (2:2). As the Scottish Paraphrase has it (Psalm 133:1):

Behold how good a thing it is,
And how becoming well,
Together such as brethren are
In unity to dwell!

There is peace for no one where there are broken human relationships and strife between individuals. There is no lovelier sight than a family linked in love to each other, or a church whose members are one with each other, because they are one in Christ Jesus their Lord.

(5) There is the joy of *suffering for Christ* (2:17). In the hour of his martyrdom in the flames, Bishop Polycarp prayed: 'I thank you, O Father, that you have judged me worthy

of this hour.' To suffer for Christ is a privilege, for it is an opportunity to demonstrate beyond any question of doubt where our loyalty lies and to share in the upbuilding of the kingdom of God.

(6) There is the joy of *news of the loved one* (2:28). Life is full of separations, and there is always joy when news comes to us of those loved ones from whom we are temporarily separated. A great Scottish preacher once spoke of the joy that can be given with a postage stamp. It is worth remembering how easily we can bring joy to those who love us and how easily we can bring anxiety, by keeping in touch or failing to keep in touch with them.

(7) There is the joy of *Christian hospitality* (2:29). There is the home of the shut door, and there is the home of the open door. The shut door is the door of selfishness; the open door is the door of Christian welcome and Christian love. It is a great thing to have a door from which the stranger and the one in trouble know that they will never be turned away.

(8) There is the joy of *those who are in Christ* (3:1, 4:1). We have already seen that to be in Christ is to live in his presence as the bird lives in the air, the fish in the sea, and the roots of the trees in the soil. It is human nature to be happy when we are with the person whom we love; and Christ is the one from whose love nothing in time or eternity can ever separate us.

(9) There is the joy of *those who have won other souls for Christ* (4:1). The Philippians are Paul's joy and crown, for he was the means of bringing them to Jesus Christ. It is the joy of parents, teachers and preachers to bring others, especially children, into the love of Jesus Christ. Surely those who enjoy a great privilege cannot rest content until they share it with

their families and friends. For Christians, evangelism is not a duty; it is a joy.

(10) There is the joy *in a gift* (4:10). This joy lies not so much in the gift itself as in being remembered and realizing that someone cares. This is a joy that we could bring to others more often than we do.

Our glory and our joy

1 Thessalonians 2:17–20

> *But, brothers, when we had been separated from you – in presence but not in heart – for a short time, we were the more exceedingly eager with a great desire to see your face. So we wished to come to you – I Paul longed for it once and again – but Satan blocked our way. For who is our hope or our joy or the crown in which we boast? Is it not even you, in the presence of the Lord Jesus Christ at his coming? For you are our glory and our joy.*

FIRST Thessalonians has been called 'a classic of friendship' – and here is a passage where Paul's deep affection for his friends breathes through his words. Across the centuries, we can still feel the throb of love in these sentences.

Paul uses two interesting pictures in this passage.

(1) He speaks of Satan *blocking his way* when he desired to come to Thessalonica. The word he uses (*egkoptein*) is the technical word for putting up a road-block calculated to stop an expedition on the march. It is Satan's work to throw obstacles into the Christian's way – and it is our work to surmount them.

(2) He speaks of the Thessalonians being his *crown*. In Greek, there are two words for *crown*. The one is *diadema*, which is used almost exclusively for the royal crown. The other is *stephanos*, which is used almost exclusively for the victor's crown in some contest and especially for the athlete's crown of victory in the games. It is *stephanos* that Paul uses here. The only prize in life that he really valued was to see his converts living good lives.

Professor W. M. Macgregor of Trinity College, Glasgow, used to quote the saying of John when he was thinking of the students whom he had taught: 'I have no greater joy than this, to hear that my children are walking in the truth' (3 John 4). Paul would have said amen to that. The glory of all teachers lies in their students; and, should the day come when the students have left the teachers far behind, the glory is still greater. Our greatest glory lies in those whom we have set or helped on the path to Christ.

Anne Ross Cousin turned into verse the thoughts of the seventeenth-century Scottish theologian Samuel Rutherford as he lay in prison in Aberdeen. In one verse, she pictures him thinking of his old congregation in Anwoth:

Fair Anwoth on the Solway
To me thou still art dear;
Even from the verge of heaven
I drop for thee a tear.
O! if one soul from Anwoth
Shall meet me at God's right hand,
My heaven will be two heavens
In Immanuel's land.

Nothing that we can do can bring us credit in the sight of God; but at the very end the stars in an individual's crown will be those whom he or she led nearer to Jesus Christ.

A singing church

James 5:13–15

> *Is any among you in trouble? Let him pray. Is any in good spirits? Let him sing a hymn. Is any among you sick? Let him call in the elders of the Church; and let them anoint him with oil in the name of the Lord, and pray over him; and the believing prayer will restore to health the ailing person, and the Lord will enable him to rise from his bed; and even if he has committed sin, he will receive forgiveness.*

HERE we have set out before us certain dominant characteristics of the early Church.

It was a singing church; the early Christians were always ready to burst into song. In Paul's description of the meetings of the church at Corinth, we find singing an integral part (1 Corinthians 14:15, 14:26). When he thinks of the grace of God going out to the Gentiles, it reminds him of the joyous saying of the psalmist: 'I will confess you among the Gentiles, and sing praises to your name' (Romans 15:9; cf. Psalm 18:49).

It is characteristic of the Christians that they speak to each other in psalms and hymns and spiritual songs, singing and making melody in their hearts to the Lord (Ephesians

5:19). The word of Christ dwells in them, and they teach and admonish each other in psalms and hymns and spiritual songs, singing with thankfulness in their hearts to the Lord (Colossians 3:16). There was a joy in the hearts of the Christians which burst from their lips in songs of praise for the mercy and the grace of God.

The fact is that the non-Christian world has always been sad and weary and frightened. Matthew Arnold wrote a poem entitled 'Oberman Once More', describing its bored weariness.

On that hard Pagan world disgust
And secret loathing fell;
Deep weariness and sated lust
Made human life a hell.
In his cool hall, with haggard eyes,
The Roman noble lay;
He drove abroad in furious guise
Along the Appian Way;
He made a feast, drank fierce and fast,
And crowned his hair with flowers –
No easier nor no quicker passed
The impracticable hours.

In contrast with that weary mood, the characteristic of Christians is singing joy. That was what impressed John Bunyan when he heard four poor old women talking, as they sat at a door in the sun: 'Methought they spake, as if joy did make them speak.' When Thomas Bilney, the sixteenth-century Protestant martyr, grasped the wonder of redeeming grace, he said: 'It was as if dawn suddenly broke on a dark night.' Archibald Lana Fleming, the first Bishop of the Arctic, tells of the saying of an Inuit hunter: 'Before you came, the road was dark and we were afraid. Now we are not afraid, for the darkness has gone away and all is light as we walk the Jesus way.'

The Church has always been a singing church. When Pliny, governor of Bithynia, wrote to Trajan, the Roman emperor, in AD 111 to tell him of this new sect of Christians, he said that his information was that 'they are in the habit meeting on a certain fixed day before it is light, when they sing in alternate verses a hymn to Christ as God'. Since the fall of Jerusalem in AD 70, there has been no music in orthodox Jewish synagogues, for, when they worship, they remember a tragedy; but in the Christian Church, from the beginning until now, there has been the music of praise, for Christians remember an infinite love and enjoy a present glory.

The final ascription of praise

Jude 24–5

> *Unto him who is able to keep you from slipping and to make you stand blameless and exultant in the presence of his glory, to the only God, our Saviour, through Jesus Christ our Lord, be glory, majesty, dominion and power, before all time, at this present time, and for all time. Amen.*

JUDE comes to an end with a tremendous ascription of praise.

Three times in the New Testament, praise is given to *the God who is able*. In Romans 16:25, Paul gives praise to the God who is able to strengthen us. God is the one person who can give us a foundation for life which nothing and no one can ever shake. In Ephesians 3:20, Paul gives praise to the God who is able to do far more than we can ever ask or even dream of. He is the God whose grace no one has ever exhausted and on whom no claim can ever be too much.

Here, Jude offers *his* praise to the God who is able.

(1) God is able to keep us from slipping. The word is *aptaistos*. It is used both of a sure-footed horse which does not stumble and of a person who does not fall into error. 'He will not let your foot be moved' – or, as the Scottish metrical

version has it, 'Thy foot he'll not let slide' (Psalm 121:3). To walk with God is to walk in safety even on the most dangerous and the most slippery path. In mountaineering, climbers are roped together so that, even if the inexperienced climber should slip, the skilled mountaineer can take the weight and save the other person. In the same way, when we bind ourselves to God, he keeps us safe.

(2) He can make us stand blameless in the presence of his glory. The word for *blameless* is *amōmos*. This is characteristically a sacrificial word; and it is commonly and technically used of an animal which is without spot or blemish and is therefore fit to be offered to God. The amazing thing is that, when we submit ourselves to God, his grace can make our lives nothing less than a sacrifice fit to offer to him.

He can bring us into his presence exultant. Surely the natural way to think of entry into the presence of God is in fear and in shame. But, by the work of Jesus Christ and in the grace of God, we know that we can go to God with joy and with all fear banished. Through Jesus Christ, God the stern Judge has become known to us as God the loving Father.

We note one last thing. Usually we associate the word *Saviour* with Jesus Christ; but here Jude attaches it to God. He is not alone in this, for God is often called Saviour in the New Testament (Luke 1:47; 1 Timothy 1:1, 2:3, 4:10; Titus 1:3, 2:10, 3:4). So, we end with the great and comforting certainty that at the back of everything there is a God whose name is Saviour. Christians have the joyous certainty that in this world they live in the love of God and that in the next world they go to that love. The love of God is both the atmosphere and the goal of all their living.

Unseen but not unknown

1 Peter 1:8–9

> *Although you never knew him, you love him; although you do not see him, you believe in him. And you rejoice with unspeakable and glorious joy because you are receiving that which faith must end in – the salvation of your souls.*

PETER is drawing an implicit contrast between himself and his readers. It was his great privilege to have known Jesus in his days on earth. His readers had not had that joy, but, although they never knew Jesus on earth, they love him; and, although they do not actually see him, they believe. And that belief brings to them a glorious joy beyond words, for even here and now it makes them certain of the ultimate welfare of their souls.

E. G. Selwyn in his commentary distinguishes four stages in our understanding and knowledge of Christ.

(1) The first is the stage of hope and desire, the stage of those who throughout the ages dreamed of the coming of the King. As Jesus himself said to his disciples, 'Many prophets and kings desired to see what you see, but did not see it' (Luke 10:24). There were the days of longings and expectations which were never fully brought to fruition.

(2) The second stage came to those who knew Christ on earth. That is what Peter is thinking about here. That is what he was thinking about when he said to Cornelius: 'We are witnesses to all that he did both in Judaea and in Jerusalem' (Acts 10:39). There were those who walked with Jesus and on whose witness our knowledge of his life and his words depends.

(3) There are those in every nation and time who see Jesus with the eye of faith. Jesus said to Thomas: 'Have you believed because you have seen me? Blessed are those who have not seen and yet have come to believe' (John 20:29). This way of seeing Jesus is possible only because he is not someone who lived and died and exists now only as a figure in a book. He is someone who lived and died and is alive for evermore. It has been said that 'no apostle ever *remembered* Jesus'. That is to say, Jesus is not only a memory; he is a person whom we can meet.

(4) There is the heavenly vision. It was John's confidence that we shall see him as he is (1 John 3:2). 'Now', said Paul, 'we see in a mirror, dimly, but then we will see face to face' (1 Corinthians 13:12). If the eye of faith endures, the day will come when it will be the eye of sight, and we shall see face to face and know even as we are known. As the hymn has it:

Jesus, these eyes have never seen
That radiant form of thine;
The veil of sense hangs dark between
Thy blessed face and mine.

I see thee not, I hear thee not,
Yet art thou oft with me;

And earth hath ne'er so dear a spot
As where I meet with thee.

Yet, though I have not seen, and still
Must rest in faith alone,
I love thee, dearest Lord, and will,
Unseen but not unknown.

When death these mortal eyes shall seal,
And still this throbbing heart,
The rending veil shall thee reveal
All glorious as thou art.

Sorrow turned to joy

John 16:16–24

'In a little while you will not see me any more; and again in a little while you will see me.' Some of his disciples said to each other: 'What is the meaning of this that he is saying to us – "In a little while you will not see me, and again in a little while you will see me"? And what does he mean when he says: "I am going to my Father"? What does he mean when he talks about "A little"? We do not know what he means.' Jesus knew that they wished to ask him their questions, and he said to them: 'You are discussing among yourselves what I meant when I said: "In a little while you will not see me, and again in a little while you will see me." This is the truth I tell you – you will weep and you will lament, but the world will rejoice. You will be grieved, but your grief will turn into joy. When a woman bears a child she has grief, because her hour has come. But, when the child is born, she does not remember her pain because of her joy that a man is born into the world. So you too for the present have grief. But I will see you again, and your heart will rejoice, and no one will take your joy from you. In that day you will not have any questions to ask me. This is the truth I tell you – the Father will give you in my name whatever you will ask him.

Up till now you have asked nothing in my name. Ask, and you will receive, that your joy may stand complete.'

HERE, Jesus is looking beyond the present to the new age which is to come. When he does, he uses a conception deeply rooted in Jewish thought. The Jews believed that all time was divided into two ages – the present age and the age to come. The present age was wholly bad and wholly under condemnation; the age to come was the golden age of God. In between the two ages, preceding the coming of the Messiah, who would bring in the new age, there lay the day of the Lord; and the day of the Lord was to be a terrible day, when the world would be shattered into fragments before the golden age would dawn. The Jews were in the habit of calling that terrible between-time 'the birth travail of the days of the Messiah'.

The Old Testament and the literature written between the Testaments are both full of pictures of this terrible between-time. 'See, the day of the Lord comes, cruel, with wrath and fierce anger, to make the earth a desolation, and to destroy its sinners from it' (Isaiah 13:9). 'Let all the inhabitants of the land tremble, for the day of the Lord is coming, it is near – a day of darkness and gloom, a day of clouds and thick darkness!' (Joel 2:1–2). 'And honour shall be turned into shame, and strength humiliated into contempt, and probity destroyed, and beauty shall become ugliness' (2 Baruch 27). 'The day of the Lord will come like a thief, and then the heavens will pass away with a loud noise, and the elements will be dissolved with fire, and the earth and everything that is done on it will be [burned up]' (2 Peter 3:10). Such was the picture of the birth-pangs of the coming of the Messiah.

Jesus knew the Scriptures, and these pictures were in his mind and memory. And now he was saying to his disciples: 'I am leaving you; but I am coming back; the day will come when my reign will begin and my kingdom will come; but before that you will have to go through terrible things, with pain like birth-pangs upon you. But, if you faithfully endure, the blessings will be very precious.' Then he went on to outline the life of the Christian who endures.

(1) Sorrow will turn to joy. There may be a time when it looks as if to be a Christian brings nothing but sorrow, and to be of the world brings nothing but joy. But the day will come when the roles are reversed. The world's careless joy will turn to sorrow; and the Christian's apparent sorrow will turn to joy. Christians must always remember, when their faith costs them dear, that this is not the end of things and that sorrow will give way to joy.

(2) There will be two precious things about this Christian joy. (a) It will never be taken away. It will be independent of the chances and changes of the world. It is the simple fact that in every generation people who were suffering terribly have spoken of sweet times with Christ. The joy the world gives is at the mercy of the world. The joy which Christ gives is independent of anything the world can do. (b) It will be complete. In life's greatest joy there is always something lacking. It may be that somehow there lingers some regret; that there is a cloud no bigger than a person's hand to mar it; that the memory that it cannot last is always at the back of our minds. In Christian joy, the joy of the presence of Christ, there is no tinge of imperfection. It is perfect and complete.

In Christian joy, the pain which went before is forgotten. The mother forgets the pain in the wonder of the child. The martyr forgets the agony in the glory of heaven. As Robert Browning wrote, in 'Christmas Eve and Easter Day', of the martyr's tablet on the wall:

I was some time in being burned.
At last a hand came through
The flames and drew
My soul to Christ whom now I see;
Sergius a brother writes for me
This testimony on the wall.
For me – I have forgot it all.

If a person's fidelity costs much, the cost will be forgotten in the joy of being forever with Christ.

(4) There will be fullness of knowledge. 'In that day,' said Jesus, 'you will not need to ask me any questions any more.' In this life, there are always some unanswered questions and some unsolved problems. In the last analysis, we must always walk by faith and not by sight; we must always be accepting what we cannot understand. It is only fragments of the truth that we can grasp and glimpses of God that we may see; but in the age to come with Christ there will be fullness of knowledge.

As Browning had it in 'Abt Vogler':

The evil is null, is nought, is silence implying sound;
What was good shall be good, with, for evil, so much good
more;
On the earth the broken arcs; the heaven, a perfect round.
All we have willed or hoped or dreamed of good shall exist;
Not its semblance, but itself; no beauty, nor good, nor
power

Whose voice has gone forth, but each survives for the melodist
When eternity affirms the conception of an hour.
The high that proved too high, the heroic for earth too hard,
The passion that left the ground to lose itself in the sky,
Are music sent up to God by the lover and the bard;
Enough that He heard it once: we shall hear it by-and-by.

When we are fully with Christ, the time of questions will be gone and the time of answers will have come.

(5) There will be a new relationship with God. When we really and truly know God, we are able to go to him and ask him for anything. We know that the door is open; we know that his name is Father; we know that his heart is love. We are like children who never doubt that their father delights to see them or that they can talk to him as they wish. In that relationship, Jesus says we may ask for anything. But let us think of it in human terms – the only terms we have. When children love and trust their parents, they know quite well that sometimes their parents will say no because their wisdom and their love know best. We can become so intimate with God that we may take everything to him, but always we must end by saying: 'Your will be done.'

(6) That new relationship is made possible by Jesus; it exists *in his name*. It is because of him that our joy is indestructible and perfect, that our knowledge is complete, that the new way to the heart of God is open to us. All that we have has come to us through Jesus Christ. It is in his name that we ask and receive, that we approach and are welcomed.

The new exhilaration

John 2:1–11

Two days after this there was a wedding in Cana of Galilee; and Jesus' mother was there. And Jesus was invited to the wedding and so were his disciples. When the wine had run short, Jesus' mother said to him: 'They have no wine.' Jesus said to her: 'Lady, let me handle this in my own way. My hour has not yet come.' His mother said to the servants: 'Do whatever he tells you to do.' There were six stone water pots standing there – they were needed for the Jewish purifying customs – and each of them held about twenty or thirty gallons. Jesus said to them: 'Fill the water pots with water.' They filled them up to the very brim. He said to them: 'Draw from them now, and take what you draw to the steward in charge.' They did so. When the steward had tasted the water which had become wine – he did not know where it came from, but the servants who had drawn the water knew – the steward called the bridegroom and said to him: 'Everyone first sets before the guests the good wine, and then, when they have drunk their fill, he sets before them the inferior wine. You have kept the good wine until now.'

Jesus did the first of his signs in Cana of Galilee, and displayed his glory; and his disciples believed on him.

THE very richness of the Fourth Gospel presents those who would study it and anyone who would expound it with a problem. Always there are two things. There is a simple surface story that anyone can understand and retell; but there is also a wealth of deeper meaning for those who have the eagerness to search and the eyes to see and the minds to understand. There is so much in a passage like this that we must study it in stages. We shall look at it first of all quite simply to set it within its background and to see it come alive. We shall then look at certain of the things it tells us about Jesus and his work. And finally we shall look at the permanent truth which John is seeking to tell us in it.

Cana of Galilee is so called to distinguish it from Cana in Coelo-Syria. It was a village quite near to Nazareth. Jerome, who stayed in Palestine, says that he saw it from Nazareth. In Cana, there was a wedding feast to which Mary went and at which she held a special place. She had something to do with the arrangements, for she was worried when the wine ran out; and she had authority enough to order the servants to do whatever Jesus told them to do.

The scene is a village wedding feast. In Palestine a wedding was a really notable occasion. It was the Jewish law that the wedding of a virgin should take place on a Wednesday. This is interesting because it gives us a date from which to work back; and if this wedding took place on a Wednesday it must have been the Sabbath day when Jesus first met Andrew and John and they stayed the whole day with him. The wedding festivities lasted for far more than one day. The wedding ceremony itself took place late in the evening, after a feast. After the ceremony, the young couple were conducted to their new home. By that time it was dark and they were conducted through the village streets by the light of flaming torches and with a canopy over their heads. They were taken by as long a route as possible so that as many people as possible would have the opportunity to wish them well. But a newly married couple did not go away for their honeymoon; they stayed at home; and for a week they kept open house. They wore crowns and dressed in their bridal robes. They were treated like a king and queen, were actually addressed as king and queen, and their word was law. In a life where there was much poverty and constant hard work, this week of festivity and joy was one of the supreme occasions.

It was in a happy time like this that Jesus gladly shared. But something went wrong. It is likely that the coming of Jesus caused something of a problem. He had been invited to the feast, but he had arrived not alone but with five disciples. Five extra people may well have caused complications. Five unexpected guests might provide any festival with a problem, and the wine ran out.

For a Jewish feast, wine was essential. 'Without wine,' said the Rabbis, 'there is no joy.' It was not that people were drunk, but in this part of the world wine was an essential. Drunkenness was in fact a great disgrace, and they actually drank their wine in a mixture composed of two parts of wine to three parts of water. At any time, the failure of provisions would have been a problem, for hospitality in the middle east is a sacred duty; but for the provisions to fail at a wedding would be a terrible humiliation for the bride and the bridegroom.

Mary was confident of him. She told the servants to do as Jesus told them to do. At the door, there were six great water jars. The word that the Authorized Version translates as *firkin* represents the Hebrew measure called the *bath*, which was a measure equivalent to between eight and nine gallons. The jars were very large; they would each hold between twenty and thirty gallons.

John was writing his gospel for Greeks, and so he explains that these jars were there to provide water for the purifying ceremonies of the Jews. Water was required for two purposes. First, it was required for cleansing the feet on entry to the house. The roads were not surfaced. Sandals were merely a sole attached to the foot by straps. On a dry day the feet were covered by dust and on a wet day they were soiled with mud; and the water was used for cleansing them. Second, it was required for the handwashing. Strict Jews washed their hands before a meal and between each course. It was for this footwashing and handwashing that these great stone jars of water stood there.

Jesus commanded that the jars should be filled to the brim. John mentions that point to make it clear that nothing else but water was put into them. He then told them to draw out the water and to take it to the *architriklinos*, the steward in charge. At their banquets, the Romans had a toastmaster called the *arbiter bibendi*, the arranger of the drinking. Sometimes one of the guests acted as a kind of master of ceremonies at a Jewish wedding. But our equivalent of the *architriklinos* is really the head waiter. He was responsible for the seating of the guests and the correct running of the feast. When he tasted the water which had become wine, he was astonished. He called the bridegroom – it was the bridegroom's parents who were responsible for the feast – and spoke jestingly. 'Most people', he said, 'serve the good wine first; and then, when the guests have drunk a good deal, and their palates are dulled and they are not in much of a condition to appreciate what they are drinking, they serve the inferior wine; but you have kept the best until now.'

So it was at a village girl's wedding in a Galilaean village that Jesus first showed his glory; and it was there that his disciples caught another dazzling glimpse of what he was.

We note *when* this wonderful deed happened. It happened at a wedding feast. Jesus was perfectly at home at such an occasion. He was no severe, austere killjoy. He loved to share in the happy rejoicing of a wedding feast.

There are certain religious people who shed a gloom wherever they go. They are suspicious of all joy and happiness. To them, religion is a thing of black clothes, the lowered voice, the expulsion of social fellowship. It was said of Alice Freeman Palmer by one of her students: 'She made me feel as if I was bathed in sunshine.' Jesus was like that. The Baptist scholar C. H. Spurgeon in his book *Lectures to my Students* has some wise, if caustic, advice. 'Sepulchral tones may fit a man to be an undertaker, but Lazarus is not called out of his grave by hollow moans.' 'I know brethren who from head to foot, in garb, tone, manner, necktie and boots are so utterly parsonic that no particle of manhood is visible . . . Some men appear to have a white cravat twisted round their souls, their manhood is throttled with that starched rag.' 'An individual who has no geniality about him had better be an undertaker, and bury the dead, for he will never succeed in influencing the living.' 'I commend cheerfulness to all who would win souls; not levity and frothiness, but a genial, happy spirit. There are more flies caught with honey than with vinegar, and there will be more souls led to heaven by a man who wears heaven in his face than by one who bears Tartarus [bears a fierce expression] in his looks.'

Jesus never counted it a crime to be happy. Why should his followers do so?

Further, this story shows us very beautifully two things about Mary's faith in Jesus.

(1) Instinctively, Mary turned to Jesus whenever something went wrong. She knew her son. It was not till he was thirty years old that Jesus left home; and all these years Mary lived with him. There is an old legend which tells of the days when Jesus was a little baby in the home in Nazareth. It tells how in those days, when people felt tired and worried and hot and bothered and upset, they would say: 'Let us go and look at Mary's child,' and they would go and look at Jesus, and somehow all their troubles rolled away. It is still true that those who know Jesus intimately turn instinctively to him when things go wrong – and they never find him wanting.

(2) Even when Mary did not understand what Jesus was going to do, even when it seemed that he had refused her request, Mary still believed in him so much that she turned to the serving folk and told them to do whatever Jesus told them to do. Mary had the faith which could trust even when it did not understand. She did not know what Jesus was going to do, but she was quite sure that he would do the right thing. In every life come periods of darkness when we do not see the way. In every life come things which are such that we do not see why they came or any meaning in them. Happy are those who in such a case still trust even when they cannot understand.

Now we can see what John is teaching us. Every story tells us not of something Jesus did once and never again, but of something which he is forever doing. John tells us not of things that Jesus once did in Palestine, but of things that he still does today. And what John wants us to see here is not that Jesus once on a day turned some water pots of water into wine; he wants us to see that whenever Jesus comes into a person's life, there comes a new quality which is like turning water into wine. Without Jesus, life is dull and stale and flat; when Jesus comes into it, life becomes vivid and sparkling and exciting. Without Jesus, life is drab and uninteresting; with him it is thrilling and exhilarating.

When the missionary doctor Sir Wilfred Grenfell was appealing for volunteers for his work in Labrador, he said that he could not promise them much money, but he could promise them the time of their lives. That is what Jesus promises us. Remember that John was writing seventy years after Jesus was crucified. For seventy years he had thought and meditated and remembered, until he saw meanings and significances that he had not seen at the time. When John told this story, he was remembering what life with Jesus was like; and he said, 'Wherever Jesus went and whenever he came into life, it was like water turning into wine.' This story is John saying to *us*: 'If you want the new exhilaration, become a follower of Jesus Christ, and there will come a change in your life which will be like water turning into wine.'

Books by
WILLIAM BARCLAY

INSIGHTS SERIES

The Lord's Prayer
Christmas
Easter
Money
Prayer
Joy

THE NEW DAILY STUDY BIBLE

The Gospel of Matthew Vol. 1
The Gospel of Matthew Vol. 2
The Gospel of Mark
The Gospel of Luke
The Gospel of John Vol. 1
The Gospel of John Vol. 2
The Acts of the Apostles
The Letter to the Romans
The Letters to the Corinthians
The Letters to the Galatians and the Ephesians
The Letters to the Philippians, Colossians and Thessalonians
The Letters to Timothy, Titus and Philemon
The Letter to the Hebrews
The Letters to James and Peter
The Letters of John and Jude
The Revelation of John Vol. 1
The Revelation of John Vol. 2

MISCELLANEOUS

A Beginner's Guide to the New Testament
God's Young Church